IN THE
NATIONAL INTEREST

General Sir John Monash once exhorted a graduating class to 'equip yourself for life, not solely for your own benefit but for the benefit of the whole community'. At the university established in his name, we repeat this statement to our own graduating classes, to acknowledge how important it is that common or public good flows from education.

Universities spread and build on the knowledge they acquire through scholarship in many ways, well beyond the transmission of this learning through education. It is a necessary part of a university's role to debate its findings, not only with other researchers and scholars, but also with the broader community in which it resides.

Publishing for the benefit of society is an important part of a university's commitment to free intellectual inquiry. A university provides civil space for such inquiry by its scholars, as well as for investigations by public intellectuals and expert practitioners.

This series, In the National Interest, embodies Monash University's mission to extend knowledge and encourage informed debate about matters of great significance to Australia's future.

Professor Margaret Gardner AC
President and Vice-Chancellor,
Monash University

FIONA McLEOD
EASY LIES & INFLUENCE

MONASH
UNIVERSITY
PUBLISHING

Easy Lies & Influence
© Copyright 2021 Fiona McLeod
All rights reserved. Apart from any uses permitted by Australia's *Copyright Act 1968*, no part of this book may be reproduced by any process without prior written permission from the copyright owners. Inquiries should be directed to the publisher.

Monash University Publishing
Matheson Library Annexe
40 Exhibition Walk
Monash University
Clayton, Victoria 3800, Australia
https://publishing.monash.edu

Monash University Publishing brings to the world publications which advance the best traditions of humane and enlightened thought.

ISBN: 9781922464552 (paperback)
ISBN: 9781922464569 (ebook)

Series: In the National Interest
Editor: Louise Adler
Project manager & copyeditor: Paul Smitz
Designer: Peter Long
Typesetter: Cannon Typesetting
Proofreader: Gillian Armitage
Printed in Australia by Ligare Book Printers

A catalogue record for this book is available from the National Library of Australia.

The paper this book is printed on is in accordance with the standards of the Forest Stewardship Council®. The FSC® promotes environmentally responsible, socially beneficial and economically viable management of the world's forests.

taken change from his bedside table over the years. I was racked with guilt at my misdemeanour and was stunned to hear his knowing response. 'Of course,' he said, 'that's what it was there for.' Mercy, it seems, was already factored into the equation.

The childhood memories have faded, but my reaction to injustice persists. We all want justice and fairness in our personal and political lives. We want those responsible to admit to their misconduct so that we can decide upon the consequences and reset the world to order. Equally, we recognise injustice and understand when we are being treated badly. So, when we perceive that our governments are treating us unfairly, seeking their own advancement at our expense and avoiding accountability, we are rightly outraged.

As the Chair of the Accountability Round Table— a body dedicated to keeping governments in Australia open, honest and accountable—and a former chair of Transparency International Australia, someone immersed in the law and concepts of justice over a lifetime, I have had numerous opportunities to reflect upon the issue of accountability and inter-secting sinister notions of injustice, unfairness and corruption. Is it apathy, human frailty or some more ominous systemic obstacle that lies beneath our inability to confront and correct these failings in our democracy? Do we tolerate the current flawed system because we recognise that those with control over the big decisions affecting us are all human, and that we too want something for nothing? Are we sufficiently afraid of some ill-perceived threat to recognise that we too are corruptible?

Or is it simply that we seek the comfort of a bit of fog between us and the abyss, that truly comprehending the lack of accountability of those in power would destroy the comforting mirage of our strong democracy?

The consequences of failures of accountability are well documented. I have attended global legal and anti-corruption conferences and heard first-hand accounts of the failure of accountability: ministers and business leaders facing bribery charges and brazenly concealing the profits of dark dealings in tax havens; private armies mobilised to shut down protests and environmental activism; criminal enterprises engaged in human trafficking and child exploitation, and flourishing; political opposition members, journalists, prosecutors and defence lawyers intimidated, detained and murdered. The economic cost of corruption is reported to exceed 5 per cent of worldwide

gross domestic product, and it can result in the elimi-
nation of freedoms, failures of democracy and the rule
of law, and the loss of health, wealth, standing and life.

In a country such as Australia, where the rule of
law is well established and respected, corruption is
not recognised as such when it buys influence and
profit for those with means. Yet corruption distorts
our markets and business confidence, encourages
monopolies, fosters inequality, suppresses produc-
tivity, adds to the cost of doing business and thus
to the cost of goods and services, and inhibits growth.
The cost of corruption here has been estimated by
The Australia Institute at around 4 per cent of GDP,
or $72.3 billion each year.[1]

In Australia, corruption spends public funds in
pursuit of power, rewards favour, and strips support
from meritorious programs. It silences journalists and
those charged with upholding standards of integrity
by depriving them of funding. Grift and stacking are
commonplace as those seeking influence infiltrate
the structures of power. Corruption acknowledges
loyalty through appointments to office and the preferencing of those within the favoured network ahead
of others of equal or greater talent. It conceals itself
through unfit-for-purpose access to information laws

and processes, vague budget commitments, the assertion of unchecked executive discretion, a quick media cycle and overburdened parliamentary committees. It undermines trust in government at a time when trust is vital to the delivery of programs to keep us safe. It allows mistrust to fester, which is nourishment for conspiracy and civil unrest.

A failure of accountability in this country has resulted in laws and policy outcomes that rob our children of the prospect of a bright future.

THE MEANS OF ACCOUNTABILITY

Strictly speaking, there is only one true accountability mechanism promised by Thomas Hobbes' social contract between the government and the governed: we give up our individual liberties in return for the promise of a common security and the protection of the rule of law. In a democracy, accountability is the means by which we collectively choose who will exercise the powers of government in return for us relinquishing those liberties.

It is the constitutional right of registered electors to vote in elections and, arguably, for each vote to be weighed equally in the outcome. Our votes in

Australia are not equal, however, as attested to by the system of proportional representation and constitutionally guaranteed state representation in the Senate. A senator from Tasmania, with its population of around 500 000, or from the Northern Territory, home to fewer than 250 000 people, wields the same power in the chamber as a senator from New South Wales, a state with a population exceeding eight million. In recent decades, governments have been required to negotiate with other parties, including micro-parties, that have no clear mandate, to pass legislation. And a vote for one party is ranked and deemed transferrable to that party's preferred candidate, who is selected through opaque internal processes vulnerable to stacking and the purchase of influence.

Furthermore, to exercise a vote, a person must be eligible for, and have had their name added to, the electoral roll, and they have to sign on before the rolls close, seven days after the election writs have been issued. They also must be aged eighteen years or over, have sufficient mental capacity to understand the significance of the vote, and not be serving a prison term of five years or more. Thus, large numbers are immediately disenfranchised from voting, unless they meet certain criteria for special enrolment.

The strength of our democracy depends upon more, however, than the constitutional right of all eligible persons to choose senators and members of the House of Representatives by voting in a prescribed manner in free and fair elections. It depends upon the exercise of that right by empowered voters, many of whom do so rationally, and many of whom do not.

In the United States in 2016, for example, millions of voters supported presidential candidate Donald Trump despite the fact that his economic policies would not assist them and, in fact, would most likely harm their financial position. Many voted in protest at the perceived unfairness of institutional structures they felt excluded them. Similarly, in Australia in 2019, millions of voters supported a government that promised next to nothing by way of policies in the face of the Opposition's campaign to redistribute the wealth accumulating unfairly in the hands of a few. Many others voted as a protest against inaction on critical issues, such as climate change and the treatment of refugees, then delivered their next preference to a government that refused to commit to doing anything about those issues.

It follows that an informed electorate will not necessarily change the outcome of an election. But accountability measures at least promise that the truth is capable of being known.

Accountability requires that we be told the truth by those in public office, and that there is a means of holding them responsible for their actions, omissions and wilful ignorance, for their decisions and indecision, for their statements and misstatements, for the pursuit of personal gain above public interest. It requires that those who work privately for public officials are also accountable and open to interrogation in respect of their dealings. And it depends upon the support of a fine web of mechanisms: a system of criminal justice and proper exercise of law enforcement and prosecutorial discretion; independent and trusted courts, oversight by integrity offices and ombudsmen; and administrative law and common law protections that preserve the separation of powers and defend against unlawful decision-making and bias.

Accountability is intended to be maintained by robust parliamentary procedures and powers of investigation, scrutiny and reporting. It is sustained by adherence to ethical standards and codes that cover the conduct of all involved, elected and unelected. It is strengthened by knowledge, including the right to information concerning government decisions, dealings and contractual arrangements, and fair procurement processes; the protection of whistle-blowers; the integrity of markets; and constraints upon sovereign risk.

The pursuit of answerability is most successful when sources of funding and conflicts of interest are disclosed, and the conflicted take all steps necessary to exclude themselves from influencing outcomes. It depends upon a strong independent press, accurate reporting, reliable recording and archiving of that record, and open access to it. It must be underpinned by strong risk-management practices that involve the continuous review of existing and emerging threats of corruption and their consequences, including favour-itism and nepotism, serious conflicts of interest, and misuse of entitlements.

And fundamentally it hinges upon truth—be it a truthful telling of our history, including those painful and shameful episodes of our colonial past we would prefer to whitewash and ignore, or a truthful reckoning that tackles political exaggeration and prevarication, and decries deceit and voter manipulation.

Accountability does not always require resignation from office for policy overreach or error, but those things must be disclosed and responsibility accepted so that the public may know the extent of the failing and exercise their vote accordingly. Nor does it require that blame be directed at public servants or those exercising delegated power, unless they have misled through act or omission. Rather, it requires an environment in which public servants and others reporting to decision-makers have clear lines of responsibility and are unafraid to offer frank and fearless advice.

For all of these tools, accountability is most dependent upon the preparedness of the governed to insist that public office is undertaken by all officers as an exercise of trust, not the pursuit of personal interest. It relies utterly upon the solemn commitment of those appointed to conduct themselves with honesty and to always act in the public interest.

THE EASY LIE: A NEW MODEL OF DEMOCRACY

The greatest threat to democracy must surely be the easy lie of the elected politician: the offhand automatic false denial when confronted, the weasel words that seek to shift blame to others or distract with conjurer's tricks. Those who practise the art of the easy lie soon find it impossible to remember the details of the lies they have told before, to distinguish truth from fiction. They become either overly careful with every utterance, fearing discovery, or reckless in the extreme, barely bothering to cover their tracks.

The speaking, repetition and amplification of the easy lie achieves its purpose: to signal support for the untenable causes of voters; to obscure evidence of corruption and head off investigation; to construct a narrative of justification; and, principally, to create an illusion of truth that will sway the results of elections, and thus win power at all costs.

Joseph Goebbels, Nazi Germany's minister for propaganda in the lead-up to and during World War II, understood the power of the lie all too well. He said: 'If you tell a lie big enough and keep repeating it, people will eventually come to believe it.' Psychologists tell us this phenomenon is well documented, and belief in even implausible statements increases with repetition. Slowly, the lies become more credible simply through repeated exposure, until listeners are persuaded that alternative facts are credible.

When listening to a lie, we can be confounded momentarily—we do not expect people to lie to us, especially those entrusted with authority. Many are unable or unwilling to discern the truth and act accordingly, despite overwhelming evidence.

Those immersed in the political scrum are often tempted to embrace the easy lie as standard operating procedure. They may surround themselves with communications advisers recommending distraction and distortion, obscurity and partial disclosure, on a daily basis. They may bully and intimidate personal staff and those in public service to produce outcomes that serve personal interests. They may openly criticise the bodies established to pursue accountability, stripping their funding and finding ways to punish outspoken individuals. They may assert executive powers that are unlawful.

And increasingly, they get away with it. Public resources are squandered and no-one is held to account. Markets are distorted by unfair commercial advantage, and trust in government, and all political processes, falls.

The easy lie costs us dearly. Those who achieve political success through it learn to rationalise the shame and guilt that accompanies unethical behaviour, justifying the means with the end. When they win through deceit without consequence, they, and we, become desensitised and dishonesty is normalised.

Former US president Donald Trump has perfected the art of the easy lie. During his time in office, he lied so often and with such braggadocio that it was impossible to keep up. We all knew he was not a stable genius, that he didn't know more than anyone else about wind farms or border walls or the coronavirus or anything else, and yet he continued to satiate the appetites of rallies of the faithful and the media with his claims. He normalised the easy lie as the way a president communicates with his constituents and authorised his staff to do the same. He punished and publicly humiliated those who confronted him about his messages and his methods. Those around him also began to lie pre-emptively while turning a blind eye to the deceit, fearful of Trump's vengeance or hopeful of personal advantage because of his unchecked executive power. Many egged him on, determined to fan the flames of conspiracy.

As the 2020 US election approached, that October, shortly after Trump's hospitalisation with COVID-19 at the Walter Reed National Military Medical Center, his administration provided conflicting information about the timeline and progression of his illness. It did this despite being aware that many close contacts— including aides, senior officials and a newly confirmed

that interference with voting machines by Venezuela, Iran, China and others had resulted in election fraud, necessitating Powell's immediate appointment as the US special counsel. They urged Trump to take 'creative steps' to secure the presidency.[3]

On 2 January 2021, two days before the critical Senate run-off election in Georgia, Trump repeatedly urged Georgia Secretary of State Brad Raffensperger to alter the outcome of the presidential vote in that state, including a request that the secretary 'find' more votes in the incumbent's favour. Senior officials, including experienced lawyers, were present during the phone call, and strikingly, none cautioned the president that the fact of the call and the entreaties for a different outcome were potentially criminal inducements to commit voter fraud. Apparently, many such calls had been made by Trump to key officials in swing states after the election, assisted by a complicit administration serving out its final days.

Days later, urged on by Trump's calls to his supporters to march on the US Congress as a show of strength, the president's personal lawyer, Rudy Giuliani, repeated the baseless claims of election fraud and called for 'trial by combat'. Trump and his proxies repeated the lies, the deception amplified by supporters on mainstream and social media to reach millions of Americans. And in the wake of his second impeachment trial before the US Senate in February 2021, new information emerged suggesting the Trump family and close associates were directly involved in a brazen plan to intimidate law-makers, including then vice-president Mike Pence, and prevent them from confirming the outcome of the election.[4]

Stirred up by incendiary remarks and encouraged to interfere with formal recognition of the election results, on 6 January 2021 Trump supporters forced their way into the US Capitol building, intent on an assertion of power through the use of force, gloating on social media of their success, and egged on by the narcissism of a failed president and his family—even while five people died, 140 Capitol Police were injured, elected members and staff cowered as they feared for their lives, and property was damaged.

Evidence of incompetence and corruption—the abuse of entrusted power to advantage the Trump family and its businesses—continues to mount. At the beginning of 2021, the United States was utterly divided in the middle of a pandemic, with hundreds of thousands of lives lost to disease. All sense of propriety in Trump's administration, all hope that the experienced officials surrounding him could restrain his worst excesses, was lost. A campaign calling for pardons and amnesty for the law-breakers gathered momentum in the name of healing and unity. So many potential offences have been committed, so many lies told and repeated, and yet so few have been held to account.

While these events are commonplace throughout the globe, for them to occur in the United States is shocking to most. We have witnessed the brazen and willing subjugation of the rule of law in a country regarded by millions as a beacon of freedom, democracy, human rights, hope and prosperity for humanity.

It is easy to dismiss the fact of Trump's aberrant behaviour as the work of an unhinged authoritarian, yet it was utterly predictable. It was in large part the promise he made to his supporters and the reason tens of millions of Americans embraced him as a kind of saviour: those who saw hope for better lives in the glib promises of a disrupter; those who tolerated the distasteful habits of cronyism and deceit because they were seduced by the promise of personal advancement or the achievement of political goals; and those who were steadfast in their loyalty to a proud party of small government and constitutionally entrenched individual freedoms.

In mid-2016, at the time Trump secured the Republican nomination for the party's presidential candidate, I was visiting Beijing as a member of a court justice delegation. Over dinner one night, after reflecting on Trump's many vulgar public utterances and actions, and his shameful record of insolvency, one of our hosts remarked, 'There is your precious democracy. Now why would we aspire to that?' Beyond expressing my ardent hope that Trump would not win the election, I was momentarily unable to answer. Indeed, the Trump presidency has directly emboldened a range of populist leaders across the globe. It has weakened the credibility of US allies, including the Australian Government, who paid homage to the then president as the price of trade or other concessions.

It is most shocking to me to realise how far we have come in our acceptance of Trump as a new kind of democratic model. It is equally alarming to catalogue the list of things he got away with, and to recognise that the enablers of corruption and the failures of accountability in public office are also nascent in Australian public and political life.

As a generation somewhat distanced from the Fitzgerald Inquiry into police corruption in Queensland (1987–89) and the Costigan Royal Commission into the now-defunct Painters and Dockers Union and tax fraud (1980–84)—although we have had to confront the politically motivated Heydon Royal Commission into trade unions (2014–15)—we are facing our own crisis moment. We are paralysed by the inability of institutions and governments to self-regulate, and overwhelmed by the sheer weight of reports of corruption and the inadequate response of under-resourced independent journalists, anti-corruption organisations and parliamentary oversight bodies.

It seems clear, in hindsight, that the seeds of Trump's America and the total failure of accountability in the highest office in that land were sown over decades. America has for the last century asserted its role of global policeman and supreme moral authority in increasingly patriotic terms, but at the same time it has been guilty of extraordinary overreach.

From early 2002 to 2006, for example, the United States pursued a policy of deliberate ill-treatment of the detainees captured in Iraq and Afghanistan, on the basis that it was necessary for the purposes of information-gathering in the so-called war on terror. The absolute prohibition on the torture of detainees was overridden by presidential decree. Decisions of the US Supreme Court restraining these assertions of power were either ignored or purportedly overcome by further executive decree. The political and popular rhetoric of dehumanisation of the enemy which accom- panied these practices, allowed torture and other cruel and inhumane treatment to flourish unchecked in the offshore-detention facilities of Guantánamo in Cuba and Abu Ghraib outside Baghdad, under an assumed cloak of morality and legitimacy.

On the domestic front, the George W Bush admin-istration adopted a number of legislative measures restricting the application of well-established legal protections against mistreatment and intrusion. The USA Patriot Act of 2001, for example, purported to authorise spying on US citizens and the sharing of that information between law enforcement and intelligence agencies. Post 9/11, a climate of con-stant fear has permeated moral, political and legal discourse in America, allowing the abandonment of ideals, the erosion of the rule of law, and justification for trillions of dollars to be spent on military and intelligence assets.

In June 2020, the International Bar Association published a piece by US correspondent Michael Goldhaber warning of the likelihood that Trump would abuse his vast emergency powers in the lead-up to the November election.[5] Goldhaber noted that the signs were there much earlier: when asked during the final presidential debate in 2016 whether he'd accept the outcome of the upcoming election, Trump replied that he'd keep the American people 'in suspense'. During the COVID-19 crisis there was open speculation that he would cancel or subvert the 2021 election via methods of voter suppression that included the disenfranchisement of those who voted by the lawful means of drop boxes and mail-in votes, changing laws to disqualify prisoners, and the spreading of disinformation about foreign interference.

Not everyone agreed. In mid-2020, Eric Posner, Professor of Law at the University of Chicago Law School, voiced his scepticism that the president would go so far as to incite insurrection:

Maybe I'm too optimistic but I simply don't believe he'll try to create a civil insurrection. I don't believe that even his staunchest supporters would respond by taking up arms. There just isn't that tradition in the US. I don't think his hold on people is that powerful.[6]

The United States is not the only democratic nation to ignore, or seek to avoid, its obligations under international law when it is expedient to do so. Notably, both the UK and Israeli governments adopted a similar course in response to terrorist activities in the latter part of the twentieth century. However, the conduct of America has emboldened other states already less committed to humanitarian restraint, and observance of the rule of law, to follow suit in chasing their own military objectives.

John Perkins' *Confessions of An Economic Hitman* describes his work on behalf of US-based multi-nationals to engineer the granting of substantial development loans by foreign-aid agencies to developing nations via US corporations, in order to profit and assert US political influence across the globe.[7] His account points to a deliberate strategy of control—more effective than diplomacy—accompanied by bribes, threats, violence, and often the destruction of pristine environments. These tactics resulted in the sovereign wealth of many developing nations ending up in the hands of US corporations and individuals, crippling the capacity of those countries to reach their economic potential. While Perkins' claims have been met with scepticism in many quarters, it is apparent that China is pursuing a similar strategy, bundling foreign aid and influence with expansionist intentions across Africa, the Middle East, the Pacific and elsewhere.

The past century is littered with examples of failures of accountability across the world. Oligarchs, long before Trump, asserted wide discretionary executive powers, protected by law and with powerful military and intelligence assets at their command. The vast profits of illegal activity have been laundered through the accounts of subterranean operatives and obscure networks of influence. Politicians have been influenced by those who have purchased access, by corruption and graft. Public authorities have spent public funds without compliance with due process, or in response to nepotism. There have been environmental catastrophes where few were subsequently held to account and future generations must bear the cost. A captive or disorganised press has been unable to protect whistleblowers effectively, to pierce propaganda and influence just outcomes. Courts and law-enforcement agencies have been jurisdictionally and morally confined in their capacity to confront

the May 2019 federal election campaign. Time and again during the campaign, as the Labor candidate for the Victorian seat of Higgins (it was not to be), I raised the issue of government integrity and account-ability with constituents. Time and again I was met by a resigned shrug. Few cared enough about these issues to change their votes. Occasionally people responded with the accusation, 'You're all the same,' as though this excused disgraceful ministerial behaviour. The depth of resignation over the state of our democracy among a relatively wealthy and educated constitu-ency stunned me. If these people did not see a way to restore to politics the pillars of democracy—trust, truth, integrity and accountability—what chance was there for restoring decency and public interest to public office?

The issue of corruption and the failures of accountability continue to trouble me. Once seen in the political domain, they cannot be unseen. Once trust is lost, personal grievance festers.

The resigned group-shrug of Australian voters reflects the loss of trust in government reported over many years by credible sources such as Transparency International's global Corruption Perceptions Index. It reflects an international trend towards the embrace of populism and nationalism. I suspect it also reflects the fact that we feel powerless to change anything.

THE BRIBE: ALL GOVERNMENTS CURRY FAVOUR

The purchase of influence ranks alongside the easy lie as one of the great threats to democracy. Bribes are legitimised by lawful campaign contributions that ensure access to elected officials. The larger the donation, the greater the expectation of a favourable hearing or sympathetic treatment.

The constant pressure on elected officials and political parties to fundraise for campaigning creates a permanent state of conflict and a necessary dependence upon the generosity of donors. In return, those donors expect to influence policy to suit their personal or commercial interests. They often seek to be appointed, or to have their associates appointed, to positions of power and to influence the public debate. There is always an expectation, spoken or unspoken, of reciprocity.

Political representatives are in a perpetual state of compromise: they must sell their party and their personal attributes to pay for the cost of flyers and billboards, bunting and how-to-vote cards, often captive to the charges of preferred suppliers. The length of election campaigns results in an increase in expenditure and correlates directly to the amount each candidate is expected to bring in to support their own operation. Most are embarrassed when asking supporters and colleagues for donations, at least the first time. This pressure creates a vulnerability and an unfair preference for those with the funds to shape and capture the political agenda and the behaviour of regulators.

The temptation to use public funds to promote a party is constant: note, in February 2021, the Morrison administration barefacedly affixing the Liberal Party logo to a government announcement, and then, in the person of Health Minister Greg Hunt, attacking a journalist who had the temerity to suggest this was an inappropriate use of public funds.[8] Government programs and services are now routinely claimed by political parties as their outcomes, with everything from COVID-19 vaccines, tax relief, regional visas, community grants, free-to-air television and GP billing advertised as party achievements.

In the United States, in the wake of the recent chaotic change of president, and as revelations of

Donald Trump's misfeasance continue to emerge, corporate donors are flexing their muscles by ceasing campaign contributions to law-makers who voted to reject the certification of Electoral College votes. While this no doubt reflects a (passing) commercial sensitivity to shareholder and consumer pressure, laws regulating contributions to political action committees, or PACs, remain notoriously skewed in favour of corporate interests. The collective influence of oil and gas companies, or the National Rifle Association, for example, can be seen to have influenced policy decisions in areas of acute public interest under the guise of the First Amendment right to free speech, with the imprimatur and encouragement of the US Supreme Court in *Citizens United v Federal Electoral Commission* (2010). That decision effectively allows corporations and other groups to spend unlimited funds on election donations, provided they are not coordinated with, or directly contribute to, a candidate's campaign. It has led to the creation of super-PACs, empowering the wealthiest donors and enabling the payment of dark money through entities not obligated to disclose their donors.

In Australia, it has been pointed out by The Centre for Public Integrity that our federal overseers have the weakest political finance laws in the country, with a high disclosure threshold, long delays in reporting, and no regulation of donors and spending.[9] When New South Wales sought to introduce a cap on political donations, alongside a total ban on property developer donations, the laws were challenged by those seeking the benefit of these donations. The High Court upheld those laws in the case of *McCloy v NSW* (2015), acknowledging that the effect of the ban was a restriction on political communication, but also noting the greater corresponding need to ensure 'equality of opportunity to participate in the exercise of political sovereignty'.

Throughout 2020 and early 2021 in Australia, it was possible to directly link corporate donations and policy outcomes. Resources and fossil-fuel companies, for example, have been close advisers of government, influencing policy decisions through direct access and appointments to national advisory committees. The National COVID-19 Coordination Commission is led by Neville Power, Deputy Chairman of Strike Energy, an 'on-shore gas producer, providing natural gas to support Australia's transition to a lower-carbon future'. Here, the conflict of interest is apparent, and profoundly disturbing. The chair of the commission must provide disinterested advice if the national interest is to be served, yet the commission will certainly be affected by the appearance of bias. Couple this with the fact that claims of Cabinet confidentiality have overlain the committee's deliberations—through the spurious device of communications with Prime Minister Morrison, who asserts he is a one-man Cabinet committee—and we have genuine cause for concern.

Cabinet confidentiality is an important protection intended to permit full and frank discussion among Cabinet members. But it has been used as a shield to permit misleading or ambiguous statements to be made to parliament, such as about the nature of the advice received, and to prevent scrutiny of those advisers influencing government decisions. It is no surprise that a committee led by gas executives recommends a gas-led recovery and a gas-led response to climate change, requiring government subsidises, contributions, concessional loans and the relaxation of environmental protection laws. Nor is it surprising that another committee, responsible for ensuring the integrity of the projects to receive climate funding, will consider the government's plan to spend the public $2.5 billion emissions reduction fund on contentious carbon-capture projects.

Resources companies have likewise accessed vast mineral wealth through our systems of exploration and licensing. While the minerals are theoretically the property of all of us, the companies are allowed to extract and sell them in exchange for the payment of royalties, creating huge wealth for the individuals involved. This wealth has been used to purchase power and influence, and to entrench the expectation that it should not be shared beyond the owners of the corporations. This cements inequality and effectively captures the policy agenda of political parties that are dependent on contributions from those interests. And the system perpetuates itself as former political staff are appointed without due process to highly paid public service roles, exempt from procurement rules that guarantee fairness and impartiality.

As in the United States, consumer boycotts and shareholder pressure have had some success in shaping corporate donations and the willingness of political parties to accept contributions. The concern is that these signals are only temporary, and that donations will flow again once any current scandal is out of the public mind.

Established parties in Australia receive public funding of about $2.76 per vote for federal political campaigns based on the number of votes received for candidates at the previous election, under a scheme established in the 1980s by the Hawke government to reduce the risk of corruption being associated with donations. This gave the major parties in excess of $24 million in public funding for the 2016 election. But at the last election in 2019, after One Nation received payments in excess of campaign expenditure, the amount was capped at what was actually spent on advertising.

Five per cent of donors contributed more than half of the major parties' declared donations at the 2016 federal election, while the rest took the form of either small contributions or undisclosed donations. One of those major donors, contributing $1.75 million of his private wealth, was former prime minister Malcom Turnbull. When Turnbull mounted a challenge for the leadership of the Liberal Party months before the election, there was express acknowledgement of his largesse among those supporting his bid. When the amount was disclosed by Turnbull the following year ahead of the routine publication of this data by the Australian Electoral Commission, frontbencher Josh Frydenberg described it as the 'purest donation of all' because there could be no suggestion the money bought influence—beyond securing the top job, of course.[10]

In the 2019 federal election, Clive Palmer spent more than $80 million to flood the media with advertising, much of which included the deliberate lie that the Labor Party intended to introduce a death tax. This was seized on by the Liberal Party, which repeated it in Facebook posts. The negativity surrounding the Labor campaign was hugely effective. While the spending by Clive Palmer did not result in the election of a single United Australia Party candidate, the Coalition government was returned. It's worth noting that there are no protections against misleading statements during an election campaign, and that the AEC does not approve or disallow electoral paraphernalia.

Under our federal *Electoral Act 1918*, party contributions and expenditure are not limited, but they must be disclosed if they exceed the current threshold of $14 299. Certain donors, including foreigners and property developers, are banned in some jurisdictions, but there is no comprehensive restriction on the source of donations. Payments have been paid via third parties, disguised as transfers to federal party coffers from state branches, or have been broken up into smaller amounts below the cap to subvert these laws. Indeed, electoral expenditure returns are typically lodged as 'nil' returns because all outlays are pooled and incurred through the political party, buried among global end-of-year figures and not available for scrutiny. State and federal electoral commissions have limited powers to police the relevant laws beyond reporting, long after the fact.

The parliamentary register of interests is now observed in the breach, with elected members 'forgetting' to list assets and interests worth millions. Where once members were pressured to resign over a failure to disclose significant assets, they now routinely forget to disclose, or they divest themselves of assets to avoid scrutiny, with partners and other family members holding controlling interests that are never voluntarily revealed. Where once elected officials were held to account for non-disclosure, these matters are now brushed aside as unimportant.

There are also weak insider-trading controls over dealing with confidential and highly price-sensitive government information, allowing individuals to amass profits from advance knowledge of proposed government announcements with impunity should they seek to do so. Very little of this share trading and investment activity is scrutinised, but mysteriously, members of government earning around $200 000 per year can own multiple properties and other assets worth a great deal of money. Meanwhile, journalists compete with dwindling investigative resources, loss of technical expertise, intense media ownership concentration and, in the case of the public broadcasters, constant and minute scrutiny of every small expenditure and every utterance in search of offence or perceived anti-government sentiment.

The government is in a perpetual state of election advertising, with lax constraints on the use of public funds to promote government initiatives. As an election looms, this advertising ramps up across all media networks, significantly advantaging the incumbent. Lobbying rules favour those with privileged access to parliament, and many lobbyists are not required to register, let alone report on their activities and intentions. The bribe also works in reverse through the purchase of votes by government spending, grants and contracting to shore up marginal seats.

Early on in my 2019 election campaign, it struck me as odd that federal candidates were making conditional promises as an inducement for certain groups to vote for them. This bore little relationship to the closely scrutinised and familiar budget processes and passage of money bills. As a seat became more marginal and electoral success looked possible, more money suddenly seemed to be available, money that had apparently been withdrawn from the campaign chest for worthy projects. I confess I assumed this was because a winning party would be able to access the unallocated spending allowance in the federal Budget, but in the heat of the campaign I did not inquire much further—that is, until my electorate and the adjoining one (the Treasurer's), two of the wealthiest in the country and well serviced by infrastructure, were promised a staggering additional $260 million to divert a railway beneath a busy road at one crossing in response to pressure from local residents.

At the same election, $30 million was somehow found for swimming pools in the ultra-marginal seat of Corangamite. And only 25 per cent of the Community Development Grant Fund of $1.1 billion and 21 per cent of three regional grants schemes went to Labor-held seats. The bushfire recovery funds appear likewise to have been directed at political objectives rather than need.

In 2007, the Department of Finance introduced a requirement that ministers should not make any decisions on discretionary grants without first receiving departmental advice on the merits of the applications. Two types of grants required further scrutiny by a group of ministers: grants that had been rejected by the relevant agency, and grants in the minister's own electorate. The following year, a comprehensive review of the value of discretionary grants, and the transparency and efficacy of existing programs, was undertaken by finance minister Lindsay Tanner in light of the assertion by the Australian National Audit Office (ANAO) that these programs were beset by significant issues. Additional reporting requirements and some minor changes were introduced, with questions of allocation raised at the time in the case of the Regional Development Australia Fund.

The use of grants to purchase votes has become increasingly blatant. Candidates openly promote their ability to deliver funding for local projects without shame. The budget process itself, including parliamentary scrutiny of money bills, is undermined by the shunting of money into grants and funds that are then spent at the discretion of individual ministers. And this discretion is increasingly exercised with scant regard for equity or purpose—in some notable cases, without apparent regard for the lawful underpinning of the exercise of power.

Governments are now emboldened by the lack of accountability to believe they can in fact get away with it. In one instance, in November 2020, under pressure to explain what appeared to be the misuse of $250 million of community grants to shore up votes, NSW Premier Gladys Berejiklian brazenly stated that all governments 'make commitments to the community in order to curry favour. I think that's part of the political process …'[11] The comment was news for a day or so. It was followed up this year in the context of the allocation of bushfire grants to Coalition seats, with NSW Deputy Premier John Barilaro saying that he was proud of what the spending represented, noting 'every single election that every party goes to, we make commitments. You want to call that pork barrelling, you want to call that buying votes, it's what the elections are for'.[12] This time the government did not even bother to respond to the criticism that followed, beyond the usual distancing of individuals from the decision-making process and vague promises of bureaucratic reform. Nothing else happened.

Some Australian states have moved to improve the laws governing campaign contributions with the introduction of real-time disclosure, lower caps, and the compulsory aggregation of multiple donations in various forms. Certainly, these measures are a welcome improvement, allowing public examination of payments. If they were coupled with improvements to the ability to scrutinise the access of lobbyists and others seeking influence, then there would be hope for some measure of accountability. A bolder option would be to ban all such donations entirely, provide limited public funds for campaigning, and cap the amount each candidate can spend on campaign expenses.

A CULTURE OF CORRUPTION

A cloud of potential corruption hangs over the current federal government due to the sheer scale of unresolved allegations, which have been widely reported in the mainstream media. As the list of matters requiring investigation and accountability mounts, the Prime Minister must weigh up the political cost of an approach of distract and dissemble, asserting that there is nothing to see here.

Prominent among these matters is the pursuit of illegal debts—known as 'Robodebt' for the automatic process involved—that was initiated in late 2016 by Centrelink. Robodebt resulted in the issue of thousands of debt notices, untold stress, reported suicides, and eventually the payment of $1.2 billion of public funds to settle a class action on behalf of the affected individuals. The government was warned by various parties of the flaws in the data-matching processes years before any legal action commenced, and offers by the Law Council of Australia to assist in rallying pro-bono legal and financial support for those confronted by the notices of demand fell on deaf ears.

There is the $1 billion government contract reportedly granted to travel company Helloworld, owned at the time by the then federal Liberal Party treasurer Andrew Burnes, with the apparent assistance of former treasurer and US ambassador Joe Hockey, after it paid the private travel expenses of minister Mathias Cormann and his family for a trip to Singapore in 2017.[13]

Grants of $100 million were provided for 'greenfields' mineral exploration in Australia in 2018, and blatant pro-coal government grants and subsidies were made to the undisclosed benefit of members of then minister for resources Matt Canavan's family.[14]

In April 2018, the staggering sum of $443 million was paid without a competitive tender process to mismanagement, deception, possible bribe payments and large debts levelled against its directors. Most worryingly, the Department of Home Affairs had apparently written to Paladin's owner asking him to resign and thereby end his involvement in the delivery of services, so that the contract could proceed.[16]

In 2017, the then assistant minister for cities and digital transformation, Angus Taylor, apparently sought to influence public servants in the exercise of their duties when he attended a meeting about endangered grasslands with senior officials in the Environment Department, without disclosing the fact that he had an interest in a family company that was under investigation for alleged poisoning of the grasslands leading to illegal land clearing. After the meeting, the then environment minister's office sought advice from the department about how difficult it would be to quietly scrap the protections for native grasslands. When advised that this would be very difficult, it commissioned a review on the impact of threatened species protections, like the grassland listing, on agriculture. When the issue of inappropriate interference with the work of the senior officials was raised in parliament, Taylor told parliament he was asking for briefings on behalf of his constituents in Hume, a seat to the north of the location of the property in Monaro, which includes some areas of protected native grasses. He has also said he was approached by a concerned but never identified farmer from Yass.[17]

Also in 2017, $80 million worth of public funds was reportedly used to buy water licences from two Queensland properties owned by a company founded by Angus Taylor and controlled by a close associate, with the money paid to an account in the Cayman Islands, a known tax haven. The licences are effectively worthless as the water purchased is from overland flows, only available in flooding events and retained on the property of the owner.[18]

And in 2020, the federal government paid Liberal Party donors ten times the actual value of land earmarked for the future expansion of Western Sydney Airport at Badgerys Creek. Auditor-General Grant Hehir was scathing in his finding that departmental officials had acted unethically in failing to advise decision-makers of the key details of the planned purchase, and for giving false answers to his office when it investigated the method of valuation. The minister responsible for infrastructure, Paul Fletcher, has blamed public servants for giving him incorrect information, resulting in his inability to assess whether the price paid was reasonable. His department argued that the premium price was paid to avoid a costly legal dispute over the valuation, with Deputy Prime Minister Michael McCormack describing the purchase as 'eventually' a 'bargain'.[19]

The corporate sector came in for its share of scrutiny too. The Hayne Financial Services Royal Commission exposed, over the course of 2018, the severe faults of major financial institutions, including banks. Many were shocked by the extent of the failings, but also by the revelation that the banks could not provide complete evidence to commissioner Hayne because their record-keeping systems did not allow for the interrogation of such matters. The commission was conducted entirely in public, from December 2017 to February 2019, and has led to a commitment to financial services reform and the empowerment of regulators.

Scandal is not confined to one side of politics, nor is it confined to the federal level, with state and local governments sharing the focus of corruption body investigations. We regularly see allegations of branch stacking and the misuse of ministerial staff and electoral resources at both the state and federal levels. Local government, with its extensive planning and building powers, is also ripe for corruption, predominantly through the purchase of favourable decisions through bribes, with little ethical support and guidance available for members.

The point is that the potential for corruption exists at all levels of government, and the cost is potentially enormous in terms of the expenditure of public funds and the loss of public trust. A culture prevails in Australia that assumes decision-making can be exercised for political purposes if it coincides with a reasonable justification of need.

Two recent examples strikingly demonstrate the corruption inherent in the exercise of federal power and the failure of our supposed checks and balances.

Subs and 'Competitive Evaluation'

In February 2015, faced with the imminent threat of a leadership challenge, then prime minister Tony Abbott tried to purchase the support of key South Australian Liberal Party members by promising that a local Adelaide shipbuilder would be in the running to construct a fleet of submarines to replace the ageing Collins-class vessels, at an estimated cost of $20 billion. The design and construction of these submarines represented the largest defence procurement in Australia's history.[20]

Despite the oversight of the National Security Committee, three White Papers by successive governments confirming a commitment to acquire new submarines, extensive and well-established defence procurement protocols, the creation of a Defence Capability Plan seven years prior, and the known interest and capability of international commercial shipbuilders, including ones based in France, Germany and Japan, an open tender was abandoned by the government in favour of a new, untested and less-rigorous purchasing process known as 'competitive evaluation'. Then treasurer Joe Hockey, sent in to do the dirty work, asserted there was 'no time for a tender process'—and was perhaps later rewarded with a plum posting to Washington as Australia's US ambassador.

No-one knew what the evaluation process involved, but it was clear the decision was political, not driven by the obligation of government to spend public funds for the best product and the best price.

Defence procurement runs into billions of dollars and is ordinarily governed by a suite of tendering and contracting processes based on established risk

On 26 April 2016, only fourteen months after the evaluation process had commenced, the successful submarine partner was announced by new prime minister Malcolm Turnbull (a strategic partnering agreement would subsequently be signed on 1 March 2019, with a separate contract in place for an integrated weapons system to be used in the newly designed submarines). To the very great surprise of the competitive Japanese consortium, a French company, DCNS (now Naval Group), had secured the contract to build the submarines, on the condition that it do so in Adelaide. The problem was that DCNS, jointly owned by the French Government and global arms manufacturer Thales, was tainted by well-publicised probity issues, including persistent allegations of bribes and security breaches. Even the most basic search of online information would have raised red flags, including reports that eleven of the company's employees were killed in revenge for unpaid kickbacks in Pakistan and corruption involving French officials. Since 1997, DCNS has reportedly been involved in five major corruption scandals, three of them reported before its selection to design our submarines—two more scandals involving allegations of murder and the compromise of information continue to swirl around the company. And in Australia, Naval Group is suspected of grossly over-inflating invoices by tens of millions of dollars on other projects.[22]

Corruption risk in a multibillion-dollar national security project involving new, classified, proprietary technology, and attracting the interest of foreign defence and intelligence agencies, is clearly a relevant consideration for the purchase of defence assets, due to the potential for the theft of critically sensitive information and for the technology to be compromised by the thousands of foreign contractors and sub-contractors engaged on the project. A new standard for the prevention of bribery, released in 2016 by the International Organization for Standardization, should have been given serious consideration in the context of a broader recognition of the risk of a national security breach.[23]

In early 2020, the ANAO conducted an audit into the selection process, including the probity procedure. The auditor's report found that the Department of Defence had effectively designed and implemented the evaluation process to select a partner for the submarine program.[24] The report made no reference to anti-corruption due diligence being undertaken by any agency, and it appears none was undertaken on any of the preferred partners either. The evaluation process, it turns out, was never intended to assess either the capability of the end product—the submarine—or whether the total cost of the project was value for money. It was intended for one purpose only: to select a project partner in time for the July 2016 federal election campaign.

Now, more than six years after Tony Abbott's initial announcement, the failure of the evaluation process is abundantly clear. Standard defence purchasing principles and risk-assessment processes were apparently abandoned. No-one checked to ensure that local jobs and materials were locked in, and few of the promised jobs have been delivered. It was not even clear that the project was technically feasible. Furthermore, the cost has now blown out, according to evidence presented to Senate estimates, with the final price of the submarines and their weapons systems expected to exceed $145 billion in what is known as 'turned-out' dollars—and over the life of the submarines, the cost is thought to end up in the region of two to three times this sum. The first submarine is not due for completion until 2032, although the audit report says it will be 2034.[25]

Furthermore, the Japanese consortium understood it had lost the contract because of political expediency, creating tensions in international relations. And Australia is now indebted to a partner company facing serious corruption allegations.

Promises of defence spending in the order of millions, if not billions, are routinely scattered around marginal seats like confetti during election campaigns. Arms dealing has been heralded as the next economic boom for Australia. Former ministers have been appointed to key advisory and well-remunerated consulting roles to arms manufacturers, leading to further acquisitions and the subversion of tender processes. Risk assessments and compatibilities are overlooked, money is spent on materiel that is ill suited to defence purposes, and our defence capability is compromised. Only last year, Thales Group persuaded the Attorney-General's Department to redact parts of an Auditor-General's report on national security grounds. The report was critical of the purchase of light army vehicles from the aerospace company after intense lobbying for $1.3 billion, twice the price quoted by a US manufacturer, with the resulting loss of hundreds of millions of dollars of public funds.[26]

The most galling aspect of it all is that billions of dollars of our money was used to save a former prime minister's neck. It's an awfully expensive price tag for ambition.

Don't Call It a Rort: Sports and Caretaker Commitments

A second confronting example of a major, multi-faceted failure of our accountability systems is the 2019 'sports rorts' saga.

Sports are ordinarily the responsibility of state governments, with some recognised limited role for the federal government in national and international programs. It was curious, therefore, that the federal government decided to provide merit-based funding for infrastructure for local sports clubs under the Community Sport Infrastructure Grant Program in 2018. Grant applications were encouraged, and many small clubs, run largely by volunteers at the community level, spent hundreds of hours—and in some cases hundreds of dollars—preparing submissions for consideration. Some desperately needed new facilities, while others were anxious for upgrades to grounds and equipment to reach a bare minimum of safety requirements for play. Prime Minister Morrison made much of his gender credentials in announcing the program, with frequent and slightly creepy references to girls changing their clothes under towels while standing in the open air.

The eventual allocation of grant monies by the then sports minister, Bridget McKenzie, with the apparent intervention of the Prime Minister's Office, was neither equitable nor lawful. The 15 January 2020 report of the ANAO into the program concluded that it was not apparent what the legal basis was for the sports minister undertaking an approval role, and in terms of the award of grants, 'there was evidence of a distribution bias in the award of grant funding', and of funding focused 'on marginal electorates held by the Coalition as well as those electorates held by other parties or independent members that were to be "targeted" by the Coalition at the 2019 Election'.[27] In other words, the funding was directed to marginal electorates in order to improve the government's prospects of re-election. Ineligible programs in marginal seats were included, resulting in a windfall for some clubs, including those encouraged to apply after the deadline for applications. Meanwhile, worthy applicants missed out, resulting in heartbreak for them.

The conclusions of the ANAO were supported by the close examination of documents, including spreadsheets, emanating from the former sports minister's office and obtained by ABC journalist Andrew Probyn.[28] They were also reinforced by subsequent explanations provided to a parliamentary committee by senior officials of the Australian Sports Commission (now Sport Australia), an independent statutory authority created by, and with its powers specified by, the *Australian Sports Commission Act 1989*. The minister's office and the PMO appear to have made amendments to the spreadsheets, including after the commencement of the caretaker period in the lead-up to the 2019 federal election.

As news of the ANAO's report broke, the Prime Minister requested that a separate report be prepared by the Secretary of the Department of Prime Minister and Cabinet, Philip Gaetjens, Morrison's former chief-of-staff, into the issue of a breach of ministerial standards. It was to be done with a very short turn-around time, effectively to second-guess the ANAO report. The terms of the request have never been disclosed, and the PMC report has been withheld from public scrutiny under claims of Cabinet confidentiality, but the Prime Minister has quoted from it selectively in rejecting the conclusions of the ANAO report. The Gaetjens report was said to exonerate McKenzie, except for a breach of conflict of interest concerning her failure to declare a membership in one of the beneficiaries of grants funding. This membership, worth no more than a few hundred dollars, was then given as the reason for her resignation as sports minister, with no reference to any breach of other standards. And immediately upon that resignation, McKenzie was appointed to lead the National Party in the Senate, meaning she suffered no financial penalty for her actions.

In submissions to the joint parliamentary committee convened in Melbourne to examine the matter, the eminent law professors Anne Twomey and Cheryl Saunders each questioned the legality of the spending. Following their evidence, I appeared with former judge Stephen Charles on behalf of the Accountability Round Table. We addressed the absence of legal authority, executive overreach, and the apparent breaches of ministerial standards and caretaker conventions.

At the time of writing, Bridget McKenzie had just appeared before a parliamentary committee to explain her role in the sports rorts affair. Despite the evidence that the PMO had been directly involved, the former minister feigned outrage at suggestions the program was a rort and was unresponsive to direct questions, asserting a number of times without any prompting that the PMO had played no part in what transpired.

This pattern of delay and faux outrage in response to questioning at parliamentary committees represents a deterioration in the standard of accountability over a number of years. Because of the elevated theatre of the questioning process and the incessant bickering among committee members, there is very little opportunity for the rest of us to discover the truth. Senior officials are prepared to evade direct questions with well-rehearsed lines supporting government policy, otherwise they run the risk of falling out of favour. So much so that it came as a refreshing surprise to hear Treasury Secretary Steven Kennedy respond directly to questioning by a Senate committee recently, saying that he was not particularly concerned about rising public debt, and that he had provided his advice on the rate of welfare support but that was a matter for government.

A number of integrity and transparency issues concerning the sports rorts saga remain unresolved. First, the Community Sport Infrastructure Grant Program was the subject of direct involvement and direction by the former minister of sport, or by staff acting under her authority, despite there being no lawful basis for this intervention. McKenzie has in fact confirmed that grant approvals were purportedly authorised by her staff without her approval, yet no-one has been held to account for this gross abuse of power. Consider for a moment the significance of McKenzie's evidence: staff members in her office, unelected and typically relatively inexperienced, not subject to public service codes and values or any meaningful process of accountability, took it upon themselves to distribute public funds. They assumed for themselves a non-existent power to spend public money. In effect, they staged a bloodless coup d'état. As a consequence, some sports clubs benefited and some missed out. And McKenzie was aware of that.

Second, the involvement of the minister, and staff acting under her authority, included purported unlawful directions to the Australian Sports Commission as to the distribution of funds under the program, and a preferencing of spending in accordance with the desired political outcomes—namely the funding of projects in marginal and government-held seats. Acting lawfully must surely be a primary concern for those asserting executive power.

Next, the circumstances of the resignation of the sports minister were said to be required by the conflict-of-interest provisions of the ministerial standards, ignoring other clear contraventions. In addition, there had been a clear breach of the caretaker conventions designed to protect public servants in the performance of their duties. And finally, the involvement and direction of the PMO in the allocation of grants has never been resolved.

Members of parliament are public officers who exercise public trust. As such, they must act in the best interests of the nation, or the state or territory concerned. They have a fiduciary relationship with the citizens on whose behalf they act, and they are entrusted with the responsibility to protect and uphold the common interests of those citizens. In other words, this principle requires that all members, and the staff who perform under their authority, should act solely in terms of the public interest, with integrity, objectivity and impartiality.

Ministers are subject to the same standards, and are also responsible to parliament for the discharge of their ministerial responsibilities. The problem is that all prime ministers are hopelessly conflicted when it comes to acting upon a breach of the standards.

Morrison's endorsement of the distribution of funds under the sports program points to either a wrong assertion of the legality of the minister's conduct or a brazen attempt to stare down public criticism and avoid further scrutiny.

As the Accountability Round Table noted in its evidence to the investigating parliamentary committee, it is reckless in the extreme to ignore the constitutional and statutory limits of power and expose the Commonwealth to legal challenges in relation to the spending of public funds. It is an anathema to every principle of good government and the rule of law. There was no power allowing the sports minister to do what she did, and yet the assertion of these supreme executive powers continues regarding this and other grants programs that are invested with millions of dollars of public funds.

With the calling of an election and the dissolution of the House of Representatives, the incumbent government assumes a caretaker role. The conventions require that government agencies and statutory authorities then avoid entering into major contracts or undertakings, and that they protect the apolitical nature of the public service, avoiding the use of Commonwealth resources in a manner that advantages a particular party. Public servants were thus potentially directed to breach the *Public Service Act 1999* and the Australian Public Service values and code of conduct, and compromised their duty to act impartially in the best interests of the public, when, it appears, the former sports minister or her office directed the Australian Sports Commission to allocate grants in a particular manner after the caretaker period had commenced.

The key protagonists in this saga were temporarily benched, with no relevant loss of income on the one hand, and no consequence whatsoever in the case of the Prime Minister. The ANAO, a key independent office with the critical role of reporting on the expenditure of money appropriated by parliament, has, since the delivery of its report, had its funding cut in what appears to be an attempt to stifle its work. And this model has been applied to other programs, including the non-compliant drought grants awarded to thirteen out of fourteen Coalition-held electorates, misuse of most of the $272 million Regional Growth Fund announced by local candidates as the result of their successful work, and $220 million worth of regional jobs and investment packages. Then there's the intervention of Home Affairs Minister Peter Dutton in spending allocations from the Safer Communities grants program. And the list goes on.

Despite the outrage from the Opposition and minor parties, some time-limited and under-resourced investigations through parliamentary committees, and some media reportage, the saga appears to have been swept under the political rug.

HIDDEN ACTORS AND THE PARLIAMENTARY PROCESS

Ministers' staff can assert an unqualified protection against accountability that no-one has tested before the courts or by issuing a parliamentary summons, despite the suggestion that there is vast overreach in this regard. The privileged role of staffers—unelected, unaccountable, in many cases lacking any relevant qualifications or experience, yet purporting to exercise the powers of the minister's office—is a dangerous development. The traditional practice of ministers accepting responsibility for the wrongdoing of their staff appears to be a thing of the past.

In October 2017, Employment Minister Michaelia Cash identified a member of her staff as the culprit who tipped off television journalists about a raid a day earlier on the headquarters of the Australian Workers' Union, ahead of the arrival of the Australian Federal Police to execute a search warrant. Earlier, under questioning, she'd denied the involvement of her office—multiple times—then made inflammatory allegations against then leader of the Opposition Bill Shorten. A media adviser in Cash's office later lost his job, and the AFP were asked to investigate the leak and forced to defend the integrity of their processes, creating untold damage to the reputation of our chief national law-enforcement agency. In an extraordinary show of pugnaciousness, Cash refused to give a statement to the police concerning her knowledge of or involvement in events.

Likewise, in January 2020, Energy Minister Angus Taylor refused to cooperate fully with the police investigating potential criminal offences regarding the doctoring of City of Sydney documents used by him in an attempt to shame Lord Mayor Clover Moore. A staff member somehow obtained the fraudulent document by uncertain means and subsequently left Taylor's office.

The refusal to cooperate fully and frankly with law-enforcement officers is a startling recent development in federal affairs. The shift of responsibility to staffers and then their assumed immunity from parliamentary processes is another means of obfuscation frequently employed, and yet there is no proper basis on which to assert this immunity.

In March 2002, federal Cabinet decided that present and former ministerial staff would not be allowed to appear before a Senate committee inquiring into the Children Overboard controversy: five months earlier, government ministers had claimed that asylum seekers in a boat had thrown their children into the sea to ensure rescue. Prime minister John Howard justified Cabinet's decision on the basis that the government was invoking the 'McMullan principle':

> The government's approach to this matter is based upon what I regard as a fairly succinct statement of principle that reads as follows: 'In my view, ministerial staff are accountable to the Minister and the minister is accountable to the Parliament and ultimately, the electors' ... What we are doing in relation to this issue is following the convention, and the convention is that ministerial staff do not appear.[29]

This was apparently a reference to views expressed by Bob McMullan, at the time a minister in the Keating government, when he argued that the head of the National Media Liaison Service should not be called before a parliamentary committee. In November 2006, McMullan revisited the issue when in opposition, during a debate about the Australian Wheat Board and its alleged breaches of trade sanctions:

> There is a longstanding principle which I have articulated—in fact, to my embarrassment, I saw it reported in one place as the 'McMullan principle'—which says: 'Staff are responsible to ministers. Ministers are responsible to the parliament.' In the normal course, that is correct, but that means you have to accept responsibility for what your staff do. You cannot say: 'They're responsible to me but I do not care what they do; I am not going to tell you what they do. If they make a mistake, it is nobody's business.' Then there is a black hole of accountability because they deal with the departments. They give instructions; they receive directions. It was of course classically illustrated in 'children overboard', but it is illustrated here as well. There is a big black hole in Australian accountability, and either ministers have to accept responsibility for what their staff do or staff have to be accountable. It cannot be that nobody is accountable.[30]

The convention asserted by John Howard was also emphasised in Victoria in 2010 in response to requests by the Standing Committee on Finance and Public Administration for the attendance of ministerial staff in its inquiry into media plans prepared by the Victorian Government, in particular those relating to the Windsor Hotel redevelopment planning process. Victorian Liberal Members of the Legislative Council Matthew Guy, Peter Hall, Peter Kavanagh and Gordon Rich-Philips, in their majority report, rejected the claimed immunity. They relied on the advice of the clerk of the Legislative Council that 'There is, in effect, no distinction to be made between public servants and Ministerial staff', and that they 'have no immunity against being summoned to attend to give evidence as a matter of law', but like public servants 'should generally not be held accountable for matters of opinion on policy, that being the domain of Ministers'.[31]

Advice to the Legislative Council from barrister Brett Walker drew a distinction between the compulsion of public servants and ministerial advisers to attend to give evidence, and the compulsion to answer a particular question. The advice referred to a convention that neither is asked to answer questions about policy 'in such a way as to endanger the necessary confidence between Ministers and public servants', but that 'there is no reason why such persons should not be required to give evidence outside that conventionally proscribed area. In particular, Ministerial advisers are not a caste which has been given the benefit of parliamentary precedent in this direction, let alone as at 1855'.[32]

It is critical that parliaments should be able to question personal staff if they are to be able to hold ministers to account for the administration and conduct of their portfolios and those staff for whom they are responsible, or 'for good or bad decisions'. With the rise in the numbers of ministerial advisers and the important tasks they now perform, including directly dealing with departments and controlling the flow of information to the minister, parliament's power to call and question ministerial staff is even more important.

A new clause in the ministerial standards along the following lines could address these issues: 'Ministers are to make all reasonable efforts to meet the request of a parliamentary committee for information which the committee deems to be relevant to an Inquiry, including facilitating the appearance of public servants, personal ministerial staff, other employees and contractors of the Commonwealth. Personnel may be advised that they are not obliged to offer opinion on policy decisions but are required to furnish factual information within their knowledge or for which they have administrative responsibility'.

Likewise, ministers and their staff should be required to provide full and frank cooperation with law-enforcement agencies. The fact that this even needs to be stated is of itself alarming.

2020: THE YEAR IN REVIEW

Our means of holding government to account were effectively shut down in 2020 with a succession of crises hitting Australia—drought, bushfires, floods and the pandemic exhausted our interest in political combat as we focused inward on survival and recovery. Meanwhile, government officials appeared to be so cowed by the threat of dismissal that they allowed the unlawful, wholesale misuse of public funds and of positions of power and influence to continue unchecked, endorsing these acts through silence.

Across the North Pacific, the president of the United States lied directly to American citizens, turning on anyone, including those close to him, who spoke the truth. Public officials lied instinctively in anticipation of his wishes, in order to keep his favour. An entire machinery of government was devoted to persuading media outlets, including social media, to repeat those lies without scrutiny. The lies in fact came so thick and so fast that reputable journalists gave up keeping count.

As luminary Barry Jones has noted in his latest tome, *What Is to Be Done*, the echo chambers of the internet do not assist in the pursuit of knowledge, reason or truth.[33] Facebook and Twitter were only late in the day prompted to delete or block users making fraudulent claims about the US election, with Twitter waiting until January 2021 before taking the drastic step of shutting down Trump's account. But the networks using social media to repeat baseless claims and amplify the voices of outrage will inevitably rebuild. The only regulation currently under consideration to peg back the dominance of online media-sharing platforms is one that will force them to pay for posting links to news and other information items, with far-reaching provisions in the News Media Bargaining Code. At the time of writing, Facebook and Google have responded by blocking Australian users from viewing local or international news content on those platforms, affecting multiple government and non-government service providers and community organisations. No doubt a compromise is in the wind, but there are no proposals to address data use and misuse more broadly, nor to introduce an equivalent of the General Data Protection Regulation framework adopted by the European Union in 2018, let alone tackle the mischief of mass data harvesting and user manipulation, or ensure that machine learning is subject to ethical constraints in programming or use.

The media has the same short attention span that we do, repeating talking points to fill its pages without effort. Few of its representatives turn up at leaders' press conferences ready to insist on answers to inconvenient questions, or able to handle being shut down. Increasingly, journalists or outlets that provoke discomfort for politicians are uninvited or avoided at press conferences. The deliberate management—or rather mismanagement—of information by hordes of 'comms' people inside ministerial offices controls the message and feeds the trust deficit, spawning wild conspiracies that rampage unchecked. We see cheap tricks and distraction, deals in the dark, blatant acts of self-interest in office, a refusal to engage with police, and parliamentary oversight.

Personal gain is seen as legitimate or irrelevant: we expect or accept that politicians will become multi-millionaires through their terms of office, and never ask how or why. And trust has been utterly devalued as a measure of fitness for office.

When politicians do acknowledge wrongdoing, it is qualified, fleeting, and clouded by deliberate distraction. For example, Prime Minister Morrison's 'apology' for the Robodebt scandal in parliament commenced with:

> I *would* apologise for any hurt or harm in the way that the Government has dealt with that issue and to anyone else who has found themselves in those situations. The business of raising and recovering debts on behalf of taxpayers is a difficult job. Of course I *would* deeply regret any hardship that has been caused to people in the conduct of that activity. [emphasis mine][34]

By saying that he *would* apologise, the Prime Minister is not in fact delivering an apology but stating a future intention. The excuse of a difficult job is offered to suggest an innocent mistake, and the intention to apologise is repeated. So, despite the fact that the media report these remarks as an apology for the hurt caused, what we hear when we listen closely is actually that there is no apology. There is only a qualified statement of intention without any expression of contrition or responsibility whatsoever for maladministration or misfeasance in office. The current responsible minister then made the glib offer in parliament that colleagues should 'give him a buzz' if they have constituents who are hurting or suffering, despite knowing for at least three years, and likely more, of the hardship experienced by many.

No personal responsibility seems to attach to any minister, current or former, contrary to the Westminster principles, and no person actually is ever held to account—except of course the taxpayer, who funds the bailouts for these disastrous schemes.

The second device often used by members of the government is to turn the attack on others, including those asking the questions. Within the mob mentality of the press pack, this new attack becomes the story, helpfully stoked by follow-up leaks and leads designed to distract from the core issue. We the audience roll our eyes and grind our teeth, wondering if we have the heart for the fight when no-one is listening anymore.

Our outrage is in short supply. When we do find an opportunity to express it, our voices are drowned out by the countercampaign, mobilised in an instant to generate social media sympathy or excuse for the culprits. Defence is turned into offence with a personal attack on the voices of integrity.

A NATIONAL INTEGRITY COMMISSION

The heavy artillery in the battle for public integrity are royal commissions and standing integrity or anti-corruption commissions. The primary purpose of such commissions is to investigate and expose corruption, and identify areas where there is a risk of corruption.

In the process of investigating corruption, a commission may uncover evidence that such dishonesty has materialised and has resulted in potential breaches of criminal law, information that is then passed on to the Commonwealth Director of Public Prosecutions. A commission may also find legal or institutional weaknesses that represent a risk of corruption or make its detection more difficult. Accordingly, it is essential that a commission is able to make recommendations for changes to, and clarification of, the law and for institutional change to reduce the chance of corruption, either directly or by referring matters to the Commonwealth Ombudsman or the Australian Public Service Commission.

In 2018, the federal government committed to bring in a Commonwealth integrity commission after its hand was forced by independents in the last parliament. A bill for the commission was recently produced for consultation, but it has been described by many as weak, with the apparent purpose of pushing off the commitment for another day. The weight of expert opinion is that the current model is fundamentally flawed and cannot meet its apparent objective. In the November 2020 media release which accompanied the exposure draft of the bill, Attorney-General Christian Porter said that the aim of the proposed legislation was to ensure that 'the Commonwealth public service … remains free from criminal corruption'.[35] The accompanying 'Commonwealth Integrity Commission Fact Sheet' stated that the

CIC would be a centralised, specialist centre for the prevention and investigation of corruption in the Commonwealth public sector and higher education and research sectors … The CIC's primary function would be the investigation of serious criminal conduct that represents corruption in the public sector.[36]

But these matters are not addressed in an objects clause in the legislation, making it difficult for those scrutinising the bill to say whether or not it achieves these important goals.

In a speech to the National Press Club last year, Porter made it clear that one of the aims of the bill is to protect the public sector, including parliamentarians, from reputational damage. He was concerned to point out that the public sector—including parliamentarians and their staff—should be sheltered from public scrutiny, including through a process of public hearings as, he asserts, has occurred in New South Wales and Western Australia.

In New South Wales, the Independent Commission Against Corruption wrongly pursued Crown prosecutor Margaret Cunneen, an investigation that was halted by appeal to the NSW Supreme Court and upheld in the High Court. No other instance of overreach in ICAC was cited by the Attorney-General. Regarding Western Australia, where Porter was once a senior state prosecutor, he cited examples of those whose reputations had been 'destroyed' by being subjected to the Corruption and Crime Commission process. I note that he does not say this of individuals who were charged, tried and acquitted of criminal offences. Presumably they deserved their fate in open court. However, it is noted that the individual cases he cites were, one assumes appropriately, not the subject of ultimate findings of corruption.

Former WA chief justice Wayne Martin has said that the extent of corruption in the public sector is almost impossible to estimate, which is why anti-corruption agencies must remain open forums. He noted that public confidence was an essential component of the effective operation of any anti-corruption agency, and that the risk of damage to reputation is the price that must be paid for transparency. Christian Porter, at the time of these comments, said he was a staunch supporter and defender of the CCC and its operations.

In New South Wales and Victoria, the process of public hearings conducted after private and confidential hearings has assisted in flushing out corruption at the state and municipal level, encouraging witnesses to come forward and government agencies to better protect against the risk of corruption. The risk to the reputation of individuals should be balanced with this to ensure there is a public interest in a public hearing, informed by a confidential preliminary investigation.

In 1982, Sir Anthony Mason, hearing the Commonwealth Builders Labourers' Federation case in the High Court, said that an order that a commission proceed in private 'seriously undermines the value of the inquiry; it shrouds the proceedings with a cloak of secrecy, denying to them the public character which to my mind is an essential element in public acceptance of an inquiry of this kind'.[37]

Murray Gleeson and Bruce McClintock said in their review of ICAC after the Cunneen decision that 'public inquiries, properly controlled, serve an important role in the disclosure of corrupt conduct. They also have an important role in disclosing the ICAC's investigative processes'.[38] Tony Fitzgerald argued: 'The proposal to close anti-corruption hearings and repress information on public issues to save those involved from embarrassment demonstrates a fundamental ignorance of democracy. Effective democracy depends on informed voters'.[39]

The division of functions for the proposed CIC into two parts will result in the public sector being treated with soft powers, disregarding the risk of corruption there, while law-enforcement officers do not have the same protection and will be exposed to the very investigative and reporting process that apparently will do damage to the public sector. This division proceeds either upon a fundamentally flawed assumption that law-enforcement agents are more likely to engage in corrupt behaviour and are not deserving of the protection of their reputations, or it assumes that the public sector is less likely to engage in corrupt behaviour or its precursors. No evidence has been produced to support this extraordinary assertion beyond the implied fact that law-enforcement officers exercise discretion in the course of their duties and are exposed to criminal enterprises.

In reality, it looks like a bald attempt to protect government members and their staff from scrutiny.

As noted, government parliamentarians are faced with corruption risks through their executive powers and considerable spending power and influence. Beyond the ministerial standards, there is no code of conduct and no independent ethical advice available to guide the behaviour of parliamentarians. Nor is there anything to address the enormous pressure to avoid scrutiny concerning personal interests, and to serve party and personal interests in exercising a vote. The enforcement of the ministerial standards is entirely at the discretion of the prime minister of the day. He or she may ignore them entirely, figuring that the storm of any criticism that follows can be weathered.

The commission's jurisdiction should undoubtedly extend beyond the power to investigate certain criminal conduct—such as in the sports rorts affair, the submarine contract imbroglio and myriad other federal matters—to the serious systemic and deliberate abuse of public power or public office for personal, private or political gain. There is a serious range of corrupt conduct and precursor activity that does not constitute a crime, including favouritism, nepotism, misuse of confidential information, conflict of interest and misuse of allowances.

The jurisdiction of the commission should include all Commonwealth public officers, namely all individuals appointed to an office of trust concerning the public, by whomever and in whatsoever way the officer is appointed, elected or contracted, and authorised to exercise Commonwealth powers. It should also cover any person or organisation standing to benefit from the decisions of Commonwealth public officers, allowing it to investigate any attempts to secure those benefits by improper means.

The commission should not be limited to investigating future corruption but should, with limited exceptions in respect of new offences, be permitted to investigate corruption that occurred prior to its existence. This does not offend the principle guarding against retrospectivity, as new criminal laws are not intended to be applied to earlier conduct. Nor should the commission be required to wait for a referral from an inherently conflicted attorney-general or meet a standard of reasonable suspicion before pursuing further investigation.

The commission should look for institutional weakness and a risk of corruption, and be able to report on such matters with recommendations for law reform. It should refer appropriate matters to prosecutors, with ultimate guilt or innocence to be determined by the courts. And there should be expressly acknowledged processes and protections for whistleblowers and investigative journalists.

A FUTURE FRAMEWORK

There are myriad steps to be taken to restore accountability through the traditional machinery, among them access to information, the resourcing and encouragement of our integrity oversight bodies, and the strengthening of whistleblower protections. We must figure out what must be done to hold government and the institutions of state to account.

It is imperative that we address the stalling of the creation of a beneficial interest register disclosing the true owners of corporations, and thus enabling corruption investigation and due diligence—this has been caught up in anti-red-tape rhetoric. We must also prevent our tendering processes from being routinely subverted or ignored, and the practice of sprinkling money around marginal seats regardless of the principles of probity and equity.

Our parliamentarians are still not bound by a code of conduct and have no ability to access independent ethics advice. There are no consequences for a breach of ministerial standards unless an innately conflicted prime minister decides to act. There is no downside to spreading lies during an election campaign or to turning a blind eye to the appointment of former ministers to lucrative positions advising industry in the field of their former responsibility.

Our increasing dependence upon technology, with the rush to embrace big data harvesting, use, sharing and retention, compounds the lack of accountability.

Machine learning or artificial intelligence is seen as a panacea for all ills, despite concerns over inaccuracy and optimisation, the confirmation biases inherent in programming, intrusions upon privacy, the security of data, and misuse for law-enforcement or hostile purposes. The scale of data harvesting, learning and commercialisation by private actors and government departments is staggering, particularly as most users are ignorant about the extent of surveillance, design flaws, and default terms and conditions.

The potential use and misuse of data to manipulate human behaviour is frankly terrifying. Accountability in this context is absent when data and data processing are assumed to be foolproof, as occurred in the Robodebt saga, or inscrutable, as in the case of machine learning replicating human thought processes through recognition and classification. Digital and consumer-protection regulators as well as law-enforcement and anticorruption bodies seeking to protect the community from cyber-abuse need the resources to invest in prevention work and systems to protect against hacking, and the powers to hold abusers to account. The US-based Association for Computing Machinery has designed principles on accountability and transparency that are useful in this and workings of algorithms. We need public entities that know things and record things in a way we can access. We need open access to data and the means of understanding what it means.

We need to be able to scrutinise decisions and spending, and insist upon the protective red tape of proper procurement processes. We also need a robust media unshackled from editorial interference, that follows stories and their outcomes instead of filling the page and moving on. We need to encourage the talents of journalists across all media.

We need controls over the influence of data harvesters and news curators, including Facebook and Google—not just so they pay for the publication of news items, but so they cannot sell our personal data to the highest bidder. Our independent monitors must be able to tell us what is going on and point us to risks of corruption. We need resources to search and discover the truth, for our assurance and audit processes.

We need, as the *Auditor-General Act 1997* contemplates, an auditor-general's budget guaranteed by parliament, protected against government interference and under-resourcing. Likewise, the resources of the integrity agencies, the privacy and information commissioners and ombudsmen, must be secure.

We need an expert, emboldened and secure public service. We need a well-resourced, overarching national integrity commission.

We need to remove the temptations for those in power, and those seeking power, by applying campaign fundraising and expenditure caps and real-time disclosure. We need real consequences for breaches of parliamentary codes of conduct and standards through debarment and demotion.

And we need to remember. We need the journalists, political scientists, historians, anthropologists and a multitude of wise elders to teach us the intergenerational lessons.

We now have the opportunity to acknowledge that the maxim 'Every man for himself' does not serve us. We have the chance to reassert our collective right to fair governments who act in the best interests of all of us, not just the privileged few, and to fair markets where participants have the same opportunities for success regardless of who they know or have donated to.

For when we give up on truth, when we abandon all pretence at accountability, we concede power to those who serve their own interests.

ACKNOWLEDGEMENTS

I acknowledge the lifelong contribution of integrity champions and fellow members of the Accountability Round Table, and my former colleagues at Transparency International Australia. It should come as no surprise that so many senior lawyers, academics, former judges, members of parliament and senior public servants should devote their energies to the pursuit of accountability, given the direct relationship between openness and justice in a thriving society. It should also be unsurprising that we form natural alliances with, and admire, outstanding investigative journalists, parliamentarians who are dedicated to integrity, and corruption fighters everywhere.

I acknowledge all those who have told inconvenient truths and paid a price for their courage.

I especially acknowledge my dear friend Barry Jones for encouraging me in the accountability project and in the broader project of a life well lived.

And I acknowledge my loved ones for their encouragement of me to take on far too many big projects, and for their endless love and guidance.

NOTES

1   The Australia Institute, 'Corruption's $72.3 Billion Hit to GDP',
     media release, 10 January 2018.

2   Danielle Rindler, Leslie Shapiro and Kevin Uhrmacher,
     'Contradictory and Confusing White House Statements Offer
     an Incomplete Picture of Trump's Health', *The Washington Post*,
     7 October 2020.

3   Jonathan Swan and Zachary Basu, 'Bonus Episode: Inside the
     Craziest Meeting of the Trump Presidency', Axios, 2 February
     2021, https://www.axios.com/trump-oval-office-meeting-sidney-
     powell-a8e1e466-2e42-42d0-9cf1-26eb267f8723.html (viewed
     February 2021).

4   Seth Abramson, 'January 5 Meeting at Trump International Hotel
     Could Hold the Key to the January 6 Insurrection', 27 January
     2021, https://sethabramson.substack.com/p/january-5-meeting-
     at-trump-international (viewed February 2021).

5   Michael Goldhaber, 'Comment and Analysis—Black Lives
     Matter: Protests Prompt President Trump to Unleash His Inner
     Authoritarian', International Bar Association, 18 June 2020,
     https://www.ibanet.org/Article/NewDetail.aspx?ArticleUid=539
     F141B-FDE8-4CA3-B1D9-A0562DAC1BCB (viewed February
     2021).

6   Michael Goldhaber, 'A State of Emergency for US Democracy and
     Rule of Law', International Bar Association, 10 June 2020, https://
     www.ibanet.org/Article/NewDetail.aspx?ArticleUid=973EB8DD-
     DCED-4FD1-B37D-573C67836D49 (viewed February 2021).

7   John Perkins, *Confessions of an Economic Hit Man*, Plume,
     New York, 2005.

8   Daniel McCulloch, 'Minister Bristles at Partisan Ad Questions',
     The Canberra Times, 10 February 2021, https://www.
     canberratimes.com.au/story/7121430/minister-bristles-at-
     partisan-ad-questions (viewed February 2021).

9   David Crowe, 'Election Funding Furore over "Backdoor" Donations', The Centre for Public Integrity, 71 June 2020, https:// publicintegrity.org.au/election-funding-furore-over-backdoor-donations (viewed February 2021).

10   BBC News, 'Australian PM Reveals He Gave A\$1.75m to Own Campaign', 2 February 2017, https://www.bbc.com/news/world-australia-38822273 (viewed February 2021).

11   Lucy Cormack and Alexandra Smith, 'Premier Says Pork Barrelling "Not Illegal" as She Defends Council Grants Program', The Sydney Morning Herald, 26 November 2020, https://www.smh.com.au/national/nsw/premier-says-pork-barrelling-not-illegal-as-she-defends-council-grants-program-20201126-p56i6d.html (viewed February 2021).

12   Anton Nilsson, 'NSW Deputy Premier John Barilaro Defends Government's Handling of Controversial Grants Schemes', The Australian, 9 February 2021, https://www.theaustralian.com.au/breaking-news/nsw-deputy-premier-john-barilaro-defends-governments-handling-of-controversial-grants-schemes/news-story/10975765e9d78f1ee34ab010b61572a3 (viewed February 2021).

13   David Crowe, 'Labor Demand Investigation into Hockey, Cormann and Helloworld', The Sydney Morning Herald, 20 February 2019, https://www.smh.com.au/politics/federal/labor-demands-investigation-into-hockey-cormann-and-helloworld-20190220-p50z4q.html (viewed February 2021).

14   Neil Chenoweth, 'Matt Canavan's Family Obsession with Coal', The Australian Financial Review, 23 August 2019, https://www.afr.com/rear-window/matt-canavan-s-family-obsession-with-coal-20190822-p52jm0 (viewed February 2021).

15   Michael Slezak, 'Controversial Great Barrier Reef Grant Did Not Comply with Transparency Rules, National Audit Office Says', ABC News, 17 January 2019, https://www.abc.net.au/news/2019-01-16/great-barrier-reef-funding-grant-scrutinised-auditor-general/10720928 (viewed February 2021).

16   Christopher Knaus, 'Security Firm Says It Would Have Been Open to \$423m Manus Island Contract Handed to Paladin',

The Guardian, 26 February 2019, https://www.theguardian.com/australia-news/2019/feb/26/security-firm-says-it-would-have-been-open-to-423m-manus-island-contract-handed-to-paladin (viewed February 2021).

17 Lisa Coz and Anne Davies, 'Angus Taylor Met with Environment Department Even as It Investigated Company He Part-owns', *The Guardian*, 19 June 2019, https://www.theguardian.com/australia-news/2019/jun/19/angus-taylor-met-environment-department-even-as-it-investigated-company-part-owns-alleged-illegal-land-clearing (viewed February 2021).

18 Anne Davies, 'Angus Taylor's Oxford Rowing Mate's Company Was a Beneficiary of $80m Water Deal', *The Guardian*, 17 May 2019, https://www.theguardian.com/australia-news/2019/may/17/angus-taylors-oxford-rowing-mate-one-of-main-beneficiaries-of-80m-water-deal (viewed February 2021).

19 Katina Curtis, '"A Bargain ... in Time": McCormack Says $33 Million Airport Land Buy Will Pay off', *The Sydney Morning Herald*, 28 September 2020, https://www.smh.com.au/politics/federal/a-bargain-in-time-mccormack-says-33m-airport-land-buy-will-pay-off-20200928-p55zvh.html (viewed February 2021).

20 Eliza Borrello and Simon Santow, 'Tony Abbott Accused by Labor of Making up Submarine Project Term to Win Spill Votes', ABC News, 10 February 2015, https://www.abc.net.au/news/2015-02-10/labor-accuses-pm-of-making-up-defence-term-to-win-spill-votes/6081676?nw=0 (viewed February 2021).

21 Department of Defence, 'Defence Procurement Policy, Procurement Guidelines, Contracting Templates', Commonwealth of Australia, https://www1.defence.gov.au/business-industry/procurement/policies-guidelines-templates (viewed February 2021).

22 Chris Douglas, 'Australia's Submarine Program: A Failure in Anti-Corruption Due Diligence', Malkara Consulting, 5 March 2018, https://www.malkaraconsulting.com/articles/2018/4/22/australias-submarine-program-a-failure-in-anti-corruption-due-diligence (viewed February 2021).

23 Ibid.

24 Australian National Audit Office, *Future Submarine: Competitive Evaluation Process*, 27 April 2017, https://www.anao.gov.au/work/performance-audit/future-submarine-competitive-evaluation-process (viewed February 2021).

25 Ibid.

26 Sally Whyte, 'Defence Contractor Tried to Block Parts of Critical Auditor-General's Report', *The Sydney Morning Herald*, 18 October 2018, https://www.smh.com.au/politics/federal/defence-contractor-tried-to-block-parts-of-critical-auditor-general-s-report-20181018-p50ad9.html (viewed February 2021).

27 Australian National Audit Office, *Award of Funding under the Community Sport Infrastructure Program*, 15 January 2020, https://www.anao.gov.au/work/performance-audit/award-funding-under-the-community-sport-infrastructure-program (viewed February 2021).

28 Andrew Probyn, 'Sport Australia Complained about Political Interference in the Government's Sports Grants Program', ABC News, 28 January 2020, https://www.abc.net.au/news/2020-01-28/sport-australia-complained-pre-election-government-grants/11905250 (viewed February 2021).

29 Parliament of Australia, 'Questions without Notice—Immigration: "Children Overboard" Affair', 12 March 2002.

30 Yee-Fui Ng, 'Between Law and Convention: Ministerial Advisers in the Australian System of Responsible Government', *Papers on Parliament*, no. 68, Parliament of Australia, December 2017.

31 Legislative Council Standing Committee on Finance and Public Administration, *Second Interim Report on Victorian Government Decision Making, Approval Processes*, August 2010, https://www.parliament.vic.gov.au/56th-parliament/standing-committee-on-Finance-and-public-administration/193-standing-committee-on-finance-and-public-administr/victorian-government-decision-making-consultation-and-approval-processes (viewed February 2021).

32   Legal opinion obtained from Bret Walker SC, Select Committee on Gaming Licensing, *First Interim Report*, July 2007, p. 47: 1855 is the year the *Colony of Victoria Act* was passed, establishing responsible government in the state.

33   Barry Jones, *What Is to Be Done: Political Engagement and Saving the Planet*, Scribe, Melbourne, 2020.

34   Georgia Hitch, 'Scott Morrison Apologises for "Any Hurt or Harm" Caused by Robodebt Scheme', ABC News, https://www.abc.net.au/news/2020-06-11/pm-apologises-for-hurt-and-harm-caused-robodebt-scheme/12345166 (viewed February 2021).

35   Attorney-General's Department, 'Release of Commonwealth Integrity Commission Consultation Draft', media release, 2 November 2020.

36   Attorney-General's Department, 'Commonwealth Integrity Commission Fact Sheet', 2 November 2020, https://www.ag.gov.au/integrity/publications/commonwealth-integrity-commission-fact-sheet (viewed February 2021).

37   *Victoria v Australian Building Construction Employees and Builders Labourers Federation* (1982) 152 CLR 25 at 97.

38   The Hon Murray Gleeson AC and Bruce McClintock SC, *Independent Panel—Review of the Jurisdiction of the Independent Commission Against Corruption Report*, 30 July 2015.

39   Cited by Stephen Charles, 'The Fitzgerald Oration 2019', Griffith University, 26 August 2019, https://www.accountabilityrt.org/the-fitzgerald-oration-2019 (viewed February 2021).

IN THE NATIONAL INTEREST

Other books on the issues that matter: